I WILL YET LIVE

When I'm all alone,
No one is near to me,
My pain is unbearable,
And no one wipes my tears,
That's when a still, small voice inside says –
You will yet live!

Life sometimes seems hopeless,
Gray skies never shine.
Reminders of my past are present, at all times.
That's when Holy Spirit says,
It is for you Jesus died,
You will yet live.

I will yet live to praise Your name.
I will yet live, Your works You will declare in me.
I am Your handiwork it seems,
The creation of Your hands,
Praise God, Praise God,
Praise my awesome God,
I will yet live!

By J.L. Johnson 1997 ©

Psalm 118: 17 I shall not die, but live, and declare the works of the LORD (I am the works of the LORD).

When I found this little nugget, I was really coming out of a deep depression. I was in church and serving in the choir, had good Christian friends, that I was afraid to share the "REAL ME" with them. It was a VERY long journey of finding out just who I was. In writing my first book, "Meet Me At The Cross, One Woman's Testimony," is when wrote "**I Will Yet Live**."

OPEN MY EYES

Open my eyes that I may see
People just like me.
Folks going thru' grief,
Heartache and pain
They just don't know
To call on Your name.

Open my eyes that I may see
The beauty You gave us all.
Beauty so deep within we don't
Always see when it's ready to
Shine bright like Your Light.

Ragged clothing, ragged lives
Rage beneath the surface
That never really subsides.
Open my eyes.

Open my eyes that I may see
The tie that binds in unity
The trinity our only hope
God the Father
God the Son
God the Holy Spirit
Precious three in one.

Open my eyes that I may see
One flesh created by Thee
Living in perfect harmony
Open my heart, Open my hand,
Please LORD - Open my eyes   © *2/27/05*

Scripture for
OPEN MY EYES

Jeremiah 24: 6,7   *For I will set my eyes upon them for good, and I will bring them again to this land: and I will build them, and not pull them down; and I will plant them and not pluck them up. And I will give them a heart to know me, that I am the LORD: and they shall be my people, and I will be their God: for they shall return to me with their whole heart.*

Isaiah 12: 4,5 *And in that day shall you say, Praise the LORD, call upon His name, declare his doings among the people, make mention that His name is exalted. Sing unto the LORD; for He hath done excellent things; this is known in all the earth.*

AN UNEXPECTED DAY OF WORSHIP

As the eagle soars high in Your heavens,
Lord my soul stretches out to You.
From the highest points of the universe to the lowest
depth of the ocean deep –
Your wonders cannot be matched.

Oh, I love You, I love You, I love You LORD.
Into Your powerful and able hands my life is placed.
Your plans and ways I may not understand,
But I know to me Your grace abounds.
Your majesty is everlasting,
You're my fortress and I'm surrounded by Your
Awesome love.

My heart Oh Lord is so very full,
Nothing compares to You.
Nothing can describe Your Holy Presence –
Oh for joy,joy in You I sing.
Blessed You are for evermore.

It's so amazing how You
offer grace, mercy here,
A place with You forever

Continued, An Unexpected Day Of Worship

To always hold Your hand
Precious is the death of Your saints
In Your eyes, as we come to You Forever.
The trumpet sounds for victory
As we enter the gates of
Life eternal never to leave you no more.

By Jonita L. Jay Johnson 2006

A WONDERFUL DAY OF WORSHIP

Fire and lightning-volcanoes glowing,
Oceans roaring as the waves lift high above their coast.
Burning heat or freezing rain,
Glaciers appearing in unseemly places.
You are God, and we exalt Your name.
Your glory is here for everyone to see.

Tender flowers emerging from green velvety buds.
Butterflies, dragon flies and lightning bugs are on
display.
They're all of Your making.
You are God and we exalt Your Holy name.

Who can look at all the wonders of the earth
And deny Your plan and power?
Who can look at Your Son on the cross,
And see His living work in the earth today and not
exclaim,
Lord I want to be a Christian,
To be like Jesus, to be a child of Yours.
God our Father, most Holy,
You are my loving and most wonderful Dad.

Jonita L. Jay Johnson
2006

Just a lazy day sitting at the computer writing and
listening to music when the previous two poems came to
me.

6:00 AM, January 31, 2009, Jay Johnson
Insight from the School of Prophets 1/30/2009, led by
Prophet Jackie Hale

I THINK THAT I SHALL NEVER SEE

I think that I shall never see a life as beautiful as a tree
A tree begun with a seed, planted in a fertile heart;
hungering and thirsting for a truth eternal, yet unknown.

The tree, grounded on the foundation of Jesus.
Watered by the reign of Christ.
The tree blown and aired,
Empowered by visions of Holy Spirit,
Made strong, steady and tall by the love of Father God.
The tree rests in promises of the Word of God,
Planted firmly by the River of Life.

We are the seed, turned into trees,
Planted in every community.
They see us grow,
Bend and flow, but never leaving,
Never wavering from the truth of Jesus Christ.

We are the Cedars of Lebanon
Planted by the River of Life.
The heat may rise, the fire may come,
The axeman shall appear;
But what our Father God has planted in this place
No one shall destroy.

By Pastor Jay

MY MORNING PRAYER

Good Morning Dad;
It's mighty nice You stopped by here.
The hugs You give are pure and sweet;
I know I'm safe, secure in You.
What's Your plan for today,
How do I fit in?

I know You'll lead me in Your perfect way;
I'll follow as best I can.
Your Holy Spirit lives inside;
There to guide me, make me strong.

With everything I have to offer,
Dad, I give it all back to You.
Later Dad, Peace out
You have a great day too.

By Jay L. Johnson 10/05 ©

LITTLE GIRL HURT* and *CHILD OF THE NIGHT came out of my time of working in a 4 -11 month, in-patient, chemical treatment facility for teenage girls 13 - 18 years old, who were addicted. You see when they come into places like these, there is a time when they need to be watched 24/7 except for bathroom, and shower time. I would sit in the hallway early in the morning, as they were sleeping. Some of them slept with teddy bears, wrapped in blankets snuggly holding them close. Sleeping, one would never know what they had experienced in their homes, on the streets. It was on a Saturday morning that I wrote these two poems.

Some of these kids had been using from the early age of seven or eight, by thirteen they often knew more about the seedy side of life than most adults. But what most of them didn't know was safety, security, the freedom just to be children. That's what this facility tried to give them back, their childhood, their humanity – hope. And they were so successful. I worked there for seven years, and now after being retired for almost three years, and seeing some of these girls who made it through the program, in college, some married with families of their own, some just living free from drugs, shows that programs like this **SHOULD NEVER be underfunded or cut** out of state or national budgets.

Believe it or not, we the public have a voice, and until we use it to voice our concerns about needed programs like parenting and prevention being cut out, nothing will ever get better. Write letters, lot's of them – not emails, but real letters to local, state and national leaders. These are our children, and we either speak for them, or our

silence will leave them open to the very bad elements of
society.

LITTLE GIRL HURT

Little girl hurt, and all alone
Visions are dead, dreams destroyed.
Hope for a future – What is that?
She's in a needle battle of
Mortal combat.

Little girl hurt, and all alone
Painful memories she must recall.
Focus on feelings-relive the pain
Be honest as each day begins.

Little girl hurt, and all alone
Look at yourself and what you want.
NO! You can't have the needle, pipe or a drink
Wake up! it's time to come out of your sleep.

Little girl hurt, and not quite alone
Open your eyes you may be surprised.
There are people who love you and care.
Are you willing to chance going somewhere?

Little girl hurt, one day at a time
No one can stop you, just you-yourself
It's okay to cry, be angry, outraged
Fight for your life! You have a choice.

Little girl, growing day by day
Slowly awakening to your own power,
Energized by all your successes.
Death will not claim you
Life has revived you

Little girl Beautiful and strong!
Growing day by day.

By Jonita Johnson
© 2005

CHILD OF THE NIGHT

Where are you headed child of the night?

What are you looking for –
pain or delight?
Who are your partners,
What do they care?

Where are you going child of the night?

Eating from garbage cans,
Sleeping in alleys,
Losing yourself to
Become one with the night.

Do you miss the bird songs,
Clouds in the sky;
The laughter of children
That sounds so sweet?

Come out of the darkness Child of the night.
You have so much to live for,
Let in the light.

The Light warms your soul,
Will chase away shadows
That ruins your view.
The Light will always swallow the night.

Awaken, oh child
See your potential that screams
To be loosed.   © 2005

I'M VENTING NOW...

As I watched the news, and listened to the hearts of hurting people, I was so angry. Not at God, but at man.

 I put this poem together this morning as I thought about the dead, the missing, and all the families who have lost so much, yet as the man in Louisiana who was 100 years old said, "I've lost everything but God." May we always, me too, remember God is still in control, and His love will always supersede our ignorance.

We have taken the natural, the beautiful, the perfect world that was created for us, and abused it. We have killed the forest; they have flooded. We have built towers on sand and expect them to stand;they will tumble. We have dug wells in water; they will be polluted, and the blame is put on God. Hurricanes, tornadoes, storms will come and go – those are the natural seasons we have. Where we build, and how we use or don't use the wisdom we were born with is on us.

OF THESE TIMES we will always speak as we contemplate disaster after disaster. I pray as we continue to design and build we will take into consideration that all we do has a reward or a backlash.

OF THESE TIMES

History hasn't changed that much,
for Black folk or poor folk
who are tryin' to upstroke
in the good ole' USA.

Katrina brought out in the open
Old issues they tried to put to rest.
Television caught what they tried
hard to hide.
Just like back in 1955.

In '55' they were
beatin', burnin' and hangin'
Blacks who were rightly trying
to live, work and vote,
Most were just barely survivin'.

Today they try to hide the atrocities
Brought on by some rich folks greed;
Levies they knew were bound
To break they would create.
The many killed
They did forsake.

Quick to rescue the Florida rich
they cannot afford to offend
those who attend to our nations
politics who's views are hard to bend.

The Bible says see to the poor.
As you open your doors
Blessings will flow.
Presidents didn't visit them;
Too many senators ignored them;
Ambulances are slow to arrive;
The police just barely tolerate; And too often they're left
to stagnate.

Drugs, gangs, and most violence
Start in the poorest, congested
Parts of any town.
Coulda' nipped them in the bud,
Before the spill of blood, before the flood;

Before the flood of violence and neglect,
Before the broken spirits
Just gave up and quit.

First, take care of poor folks
Here at home,
Nip the problems in the bud.
Problems don't multiply as fast
When they're dealt with and recognized.

You're being advised, take some pride.
Stop tryin' to hide or forget
Where most of our talent, genius
And national icons come from –
In the poorest parts of town and country
Reside.
God Bless the USA.

By Jay Johnson ©

HOLY LORD

You are Holy Lord, surround my life in You.
Let the presence of Your Holy love fill my life anew.
Be near me as I journey through temptations small and
great.
Clean me daily this I pray, restore my strength and faith.
I'm not perfect or complete until I rest in You.

Your Word I seek to follow.
Your ways will lead me on.
You are the Light who guides my steps.
Open my eyes to see Your wonders everyday,
Your beauty as I go.

Into each life that comes my way,
Allow Your love to show;
So they may see Your love in me
And know Your mercy true,
And desire you as I do.

Holy, Holy, Holy Lord surround my life in You.

MAY 12, 2008

GOD IS GREAT, GOD IS GOOD

God is great, God is good...
Does He really know I'm here?
Sometimes I wonder
Does He care?
My life seems to be going nowhere.

God is great, God is Good...
Day and night these words abound
In my mind
On my tongue
In my spirit I hear the sounds

God is great and
God is good...

In sickness and in health
In want or in wealth,
And even in those times of doubt
I know I'll grow in His favor
Cause'
My soul will sing these words forever...

GOD IS GREAT, GOD IS GOOD
...GOD IS GREAT, GOD IS GOOD
...GOD IS GREAT,
GOD IS GOOD...
and all the time GOD IS GOOD!

By Jonita Johnson

WE ARE ONE
A marriage poem written for a friend who is now in the arms of our Lord Jesus

We've stood alone by time and miles;
Today we are together,
United as One in Christ;
Our love is forever,
And in our Lord we stand;
Always united in heart and hand.

©By
Jay Johnson July 7, 2008

LOST IN SILENCE

My soul was lost in silence
My feet were stuck in clay
My mouth was set against the Lord above
I found no other way

Pride was my clothing
Corruption took my mind
I prospered greatly in wicked deeds
I never knew my need

One day I passed a church
It seemed to call me in
I fell down on my knees and cried
Do You REALLY know I'm here?

What do You want from me
I have nothing left to give
Then I heard a small voice say
"I came to give you joy.

I'm here so you will know the peace
I left for you.
I'm here so you will know
I died for love of you.
I'm here so you would know
There is a plan for you.
I'm here to fulfill my Father's love
and His perfect plan."

continued

Continued - Lost In silence

In you there is hope
For those who only know failure
In you there is contentment
For those who only sought greed
In you the world will see how
I make all things new.
Your old is passed away,
a new babe in Me you'll grow.

You're offered today the gift of grace,
A pardon full and free
You're offered today a brand new life.
Accept or reject, the choice is yours
But this one thing please know.

I've counted all your tears,
And watched you run in fear.
There's not a time when you were hurt,
That I didn't see you through.
I made a way for you to escape,
Grow, and live to tell
That in this life, tho' filled with pain
you are not alone.

September 12, 2008

MY CANVAS
March 2005

Just as I open my eyes to the dawn
The colors are gorgeous, as I give a yawn.

What will I make of this perfect gift?
A canvas that's empty placed right
In front.

I'm in charge of the choices I make.
I have the power to destroy or create –
My destiny.

Will my canvas lift the hearts of those who see?
Will they be in despair and shake their heads?
Pink laughing, yellow delight
Blacks and grays – tornado swirls
My voice
My choice.
What of my canvas will I make?

By Jonita L. Johnson © 2005

We have been blessed in the Northwest to have a man so talented as a pianist. Frank loves the Lord, and uses his talents to bring so much joy to the world around. When he plays in the Alzheimer units, the patients just beam as they remember, and they always ask me, "Is that young man coming back?"

Our Magic Fingered Man

Some folks do things for money
It's always, "What's in it for me?"
Some folks have good intentions, but
Always miss the mark
Of where they're called to be.

Then there are others who are good to their word
Integrity is born within
Loyalty engulfs their soul
And takes them to their goals.

One man stands among us
Who is faithful to his call.
He's not a man of greed or conceit,
And being *ALL THAT* is not his need.

His Magic Fingers produce amazing sounds
As he works the ivories, blacks and whites
Love for the Lord, mankind and his craft
Propels him into action
And is our delight,
That's a fact.

Tonight, our love goes out to say Thank You Frank,
Our Magic Fingered Man.   2009

For my grandson Marcus
WHAT MAKES A WARRIOR

A Warrior has the ability to distinguish
Right from wrong;
Good from evil.
A Warrior has the courage to stand
Through fear for a cause that will
help and not hurt.

A Warrior has compassion for his family,
Community, his nation and the world.
A Warrior is loyal, selfless, strong – yet meek.

A Warrior can endure and not stoop to levels
Of those who are
Out for themselves.
A Warrior seeks to live in peace
With all men,
As much as is within himself.
A Christian Warrior loves the Lord
And the Bible will be his WORD.

Your Birthday brings back so many memories for me. I was there to hold you, and to watch you grow; to give you cookies, cake; and watch you make a mess fixing fresh cranberry sauce with your dad and uncles for Thanksgiving dinner; to watch you at two look in awe at the many Christmas trees, and pick out your favorite. I remember you going caroling on Christmas eve, and laughing in wholehearted peacefulness as people opened their doors to listen to us sing off tune Christmas songs.

Continued

Continued – What Makes A Warrior

Yes, your birthday is special – just as you are.
Grandson, I love you so very much. I drew this picture
for you because you are the embodiment of strength.
You are strong, and will get through this time. And I am
sure in time will be able to use this experience to help
others.

HOLY, HOLY

Holy, Holy Spirit
Holy, Holy Dove
Holy, Holy Father
Holy, Holy Love
Holy, Holy Presence
Come into this place

Take away the sadness
Drive away the pain

Holy, Holy Jesus
You are my first love
Knead me, mold me, make me
Wrap me in Your love.

9/16/09   By Jonita Johnson

PUPPET

Up and down
Twirl around
Like a puppet on a string

Speak
Sit
Smile and Grin
It's so easy to inter-blend

Crossway
Stowaway
Breakaway
I'll walk away TODAY!!!

916/09
By Jonita L. Johnson

Puppets we do not have to be. What will you walk away
from today?

...THEN CAME JESUS
John15:

...Then came Jesus into my life one night.

I sat on my bed of trouble.
Pained, distressed, ashamed, a mess

...Then came Jesus and told me -
I was clean.

I didn't really believe Him
But He refused to leave.

He told me of His love for me.
I said, "Why should I believe?"

He said, "Because I gave My life for you, I'm with You
in this room.
You cannot escape My love
I have a plan for you
I chose you before the world began
I'll love you to your end."

Everyday when I awake -
No matter the road I take
Jesus comes, takes my hand
And leads me safely on.

9/17/09   Jonita Johnson

YOU SAID!

You said to be holy
Just as You are
You said be perfect
And walk each day in faith.
It is by grace that
You will lead today.

Where You lead me I will follow
Where You guide me I will go
To my sister who hurts so bad
Let me reach her, show her You.
And let hope be in her view.

The just shall walk by faith, You said
Let my brother see Your grace
Teach him wisdom, work and praise.
You are the son, father, friend and brother
For him to follow where there is no other.

9/17/09
By Jonita Johnson

MOST HIGH GOD YOU ARE

Holy, Holy, Holy
Most High God You are
Ever will I praise Your name
Unto me You came

So many times I stumble
So many times I fall
Yet, You've never left me
You're lifting when I fall

Holy, Holy, Holy
Most High God You are
Ever will I praise Your name
Your light put sin to shame

Your light awaits to lead me
Your light does guide my way
You take away the darkness
When the shadows block my way

Holy, Holy, Holy
Most High God You are
Ever will I praise Your name
Your Spirit cries out Your fame

Holy, Holy Spirit
Holy, Holy Dove
Holy, Holy Father
Lift me on wings of love
Hide me in Your Mercy
Grant me grace and favor Holy, Holy Love - 2009

For Mama Heath in Seattle   10/26/2009 @ 6:30 AM
EARLY IN THE MORNING

Early in the morning before the light of day
You meet me, and You welcome me
Into Your presence,
It's here I want to stay.
At every roadblock of my life
You've made a way and
Today I just want to say
I love You!

I love You for Your plan for me
Before the world began.
I love You for Your healing me...
... As sickness turned to sin
I love You for trusting me...
...with the lives of helpless babes
I love You for raising them...
...despite of me in the way
I love You for what You taught me -
So I could teach them - to see You
And they would come to You

I love You for the sunshine
That warms me when I'm cold
I love you for the rain
That helps the flowers grow
I love You even for the cold
That brings rest and rebirth
I love You when the storms of life roll in
You're here to take my hand - *Continued*

Continued, Early In The Morning

And when this life is over
And here I'll no longer stand,
No longer will I walk this earth

It is with You I'll travel
Through eternity Brand New
Oh, I love You precious Savior
Your face I long to see
And early in the morning,
hear the words from You to me –
Well Done My Child,
Enter In And Dwell With ME!!

By, Jonita Johnson

TOUCH, TOUCH ME LORD JESUS

I was wounded, torn, hurt, and tired
Searching for a safe place,
- Someone
Somewhere to run and hide.

Not trusting
I learned to play a game
A game of make believe
That takes on a form of reality
Really a penalty.

Who Am I Now?

Many faces I put on
Survival comes in many forms.
I've learned them well
I have Survived.

I've learned to become many people,
but me I've somehow lost.

Where is this God you say
Can make me whole,
Heal my pain,
Bring me joy,
Help me know myself again?

Continued

Continued, Touch, Touch Me Lord

Touch me.
Touch **ME** Lord Jesus
Show me who I am

Please, remove the masks
Forever

November 11, 2009
By Jonita L. Jay Johnson

SINCE JESUS CAME

Since Jesus came
My life has not been the same
Since Jesus came
My life is not mundane.

Since Jesus came
He's washed away my pain
Since Jesus came
I'm not the same.

My anger has been turned to joy
His Word replaced confusion
His presence takes away all fear
I'm so thankful He's always near.

Since Jesus Came
I can't go back
I'm under His blood
Showered with His love.

Since Jesus came
My heart is fixed
My mind's made up
My life's been changed
Victory for me, prearranged

Since Jesus came into my life
I walk in His authority
I live in His promise
I depend upon His Word.

Continued, Since Jesus Came

Since Jesus came
I've learned to lean on Him
Follow His lead
Plant His seeds.

By Jonita L. Jay Johnson
November 19, 2009

STARLIGHT
9/16/09

Starlight – star bright
I have never been a light
Only clouds, dark and scary
Surround me in the night.

Starlight – star bright
All the stars I see tonight
make me shine
Become a light
Bringing laughter, joy and glee.

Wish I may
Wish I might
Be someones light tonight.

By Pastor Jay Johnson

HOLD ON, BE STRONG!
For my daughter Dee

Many days and nights I cried myself to sleep
Thoughts of suicide flowing in my mind –
DEPRESSION
Many days and nights I thought I was alone
Thinking there's no way to make it on my own –
DOUBT
But LORD you moved the heavens, sent Your angels
Especially to me, just to give me **HOPE**
HOLD ON, <u>DON'T QUIT</u>
HOLD ON, BE STRONG
YOU CAN MAKE IT THROUGH THIS STORM
Just like gold you're being redefined
As the waste falls from silver – **BY FIRE**
Your strength is being born
HOLD ON, BE STRONG
Father's love will guide you on
Look to Him who knows your ways
Look to Him who knows your name
Look to Him who knows your pain
He really does see your tears
HOLD ON, BE STRONG
my daughter, my baby girl
There's a rainbow of blessings
Waiting...
And bunches of prayers
being prayed just for you.

JUST HOLD ON, DON'T QUIT!
I love you, Mama
- November 26, 2009

HOLY MOMENTS

Holy Moments past and new
Awaits the wonders of
Life Anew

How Often we give in
Relinquish our dreams
Fold under pressure
When new dreams begin

Holy Moments
Given by God
To experience the wonder
Of His love from above

Holy Moments
From bursts of colors
In powerful sunsets
A nose touched by dandelions
Or the smell of a rose

Holy moments
Through the eyes of a child
Or in a grandma's smile

Thank You Father
For moments so holy
Wonderful and true.
December 2009

SEARCH ME

Search me, try me
Cleanse me today

Make me your vessel
Molded to be used
Refined by Your fire
You've made me brand new

Search me and try me
Master today
I'll Sing of Your love
Praise You always

7/3/2010 by Jonita Johnson

PRAISE TO JEHOVAH

Praise to Jehovah, my God my Rock
Praise to Jehovah, Who keeps me and heals
Praise to Jehovah, who calms me still
Praise to Jehovah, turns bitter to sweet
Praise to Jehovah, a lamp to my feet.

Sweet Holy Spirit
Sweet Lamb of God
Jesus my Savior
Dwell in me now
Stay in my heart
Make me Your vessel
Praise to Jehovah, in me You dwell

By Jonita (Jay) Johnson
July 3, 2010

I NEED YOU LORD

I need You Lord to guide my every step
I need You Lord to light my way

I need You Lord to fill my heart with love
To show to others
How You've changed me with Your love

I need You Lord to make the life I sing about
Powerful and brilliant

I need You Lord to take my hand
Extend the touch
To those You love so much

I need You Lord to wrap in love
Those who feel so far from You
Hold them close
Let them know
It was for them Your precious blood did flow

by Jonita Johnson
July 3, 2010

GREAT IS YOUR FAITHFULNESS

Great is Your faithfulness
Peace ever flowing
Keep me from falling
Away from Your love

Great is Your mercy
Your love is mighty
Who but You Almighty God
Is able to save from mighty floods?

Where sin prevails
Your grace prevails
Where hate assails
Your power cast down
Where death destroys
Your love surrounds

Like a mighty river flowing
My life in You is growing
Transforming and renewing
Your faithfulness I see

Great is Your faithfulness
Your mercy new each morning
Great is Your faithfulness
Your love endures forever
Great is Your faithfulness
Your face I long to see
GREAT IS YOUR FAITHFULNESS
GREAT IS YOUR FAITHFULNESS...
by Jonita L. Johnson - July 2, 2010

I LIFT MY EYES TO YOU ALONE

My sight is failing
My teeth are gone
My hearing's faulty
And my strength is almost gone
My sleep is shortened
My steps I calculate
My hair has turned from dark to gray
My mind sometimes goes astray

BUT, through it all
I give You praise
You've kept my will
To serve You still
I lift my eyes to You

I lift my eyes to You alone
Your image never changes
You, my Lord are constant
Your promises to me remain always true
So I lift my eyes to You

Your love
Your grace
Your mercy is always in my view
You speak to me – I hear Your voice
You guide me by Your powerful hand
I'll never doubt Your touch.

Continued

Continued, I Lift My Eyes To You Lord

Though my hair is gray and woolly
Your Word to me is true
I'll be fruitful and multiply
Teaching others to follow You

By Pastor Jonita L. (Jay) Johnson
July 2, 2010

Somebody prayed for me had me on their mind,
took the time to pray for me.
I'm so glad they prayed, I'm so glad they prayed,
I'm so glad they prayed for me.

I am 65 years old, and many years ago the old folks in my life prayed for me – even tho' I told them not too. Who wouldn't want prayer? Well, every time those folks started prayin' for me my life of sin and fun would start to go topsy turvy. Nothing seemed to go right in my planning and scheming. Now, I'm so glad they didn't give up on me, and leave me to my own devises and misplaced wishes.

Never in my life have I or do I consider myself a poet, but the Lord has blessed me in these later years with a few words that have become dear to my heart, and I hope they speak to yours. Any of the books I have or will write include scripture. Most of the poems were written during my morning devotion time. I love going to that quiet place with where the Holy Spirit meets me first thing in the morning. There is power and comfort in the Word. So if you don't like the poetry, please read the scriptures.

Thank you for supporting this effort, and **MUCH LOVE TO YOU ALL!!**

Teach me, Oh LORD to follow every one of Your
Principles.
Give me understanding and I will obey Your law;
I will put it into practice with all my heart.
Make me walk along the path of Your commands,
For that is where my happiness is found.
Give me an eagerness for Your decrees;
do not inflict me with love for money!
Turn my eyes from worthless things,
and give me life through Your Word.
Reassure me of Your promise,
which is for those who honor you.
I long to obey Your commandments!
Renew my life with Your goodness.
LORD give to me Your unfailing love,
The salvation that you promised me.
Then I will have an answer for those who taunt me,
For I trust in Your Word.

Psalm

119:33-42

This is poetry at its best, and I didn't write it. I discovered this writing when I was a very rebellious teenager. I showed it to an adult in my life, and their words to me was something to the effect of, unless I change my ways, it won't happen. Well, off and on throughout my young adult life I tried to change, but it wasn't happening much. There has always been an undercurrent of rebelliousness in me, the need to do it my way. Eventually I forgot about this passage altogether.

But as God would have it, He brought it back. I learned that even as a teenager when no one else could see Him working in me, He was pulling me, implanting His Word, allowing my desire for Him to form in my inner parts. All those prayers that my family was praying wasn't landing on deaf ears – God's not deaf, nor does He forget His plan and purpose for us that He created us to live in.

If you have a scripture that is near and dear to your heart, and you don't know Jesus as yet. He's working it out for you.

THE WOMEN GATHER

Black and White and sometimes Yellow,
They gather to laugh, cry, and sometimes
Stretch the truth into laughable lies.
Yes, they gather in good and the bad times,
And always in sad and grieving times.
Their knowledge of love for life and each other,
Form unbreakable bonds that years and miles,
And changes in life will never destroy.

The little women gather, while watching the large,
Imitating who they will become
and what they are to say and do.
The little women learn the feelings
that go with unsaid words.

The women will always gather
forming worldwide bonds that
Defy color, culture, religion or race.

The women gather as one in mind
And one in heart.
The women gather, always they gather….
There'll never be a day
When the women cease to gather.

By Jonita Johnson © 1997

Made in the USA
Monee, IL
07 July 2026

56550232R00030